ELIZABETHAN

XII

JONATHAN LOVEJOY

Jonathan Lovejoy

ELIZABETHAN

The Complete Poems of Elizabeth Peele

❦

Volume XII

Jonathan Lovejoy

✝ Armageddon Publishing

Cover: *After the Bath*, 1894
William Adolph Bouguereau (1825-1905)

ISBN-10: 0692355693
ISBN-13: 978-0692355695

For every Elizabeth

Introduction

Carmen Angelina Coletti (Elizabeth Peele) was perhaps the greatest composer who ever lived. After her death, studies of her music revealed a body of work—almost exclusively instrumental—of such beauty and power as to defy description. Even so, her lifelong reclusiveness rendered them obsolete to the world, and these musical treasures may remain apart from public view forever.

Even those few who heard her original scores did so in quiet apprehension, that this beautiful widow—lost somewhere deep in North Carolina farming country—brought forth music as completely ingenious as any ever written before. The sounds of greatness flowing from this woman's piano, surely this is not meant to be! For what purpose can she truly serve as a neoclassical composer in a jaded modern world, except as a curiosity and eventually, a fountain of eternal exploitation?

But while music did serve as a profession for her since she was twelve—her only wage being a sound mind and spirit—there was still another expression, both private and unintentional, equally meant for her eyes only. Gathered posthumously, so few of these "assemblies" can be called unique or special, and likely cannot set her apart from any other lonely poet in the world. But still they live on, as a glimpse into the mind of a musical genius and abused woman of Faith. Written parallel to her music over the years—with no striving for greatness or immortality—these poetic trifles, ironically, may be the only compositions of hers the world will ever hear.

Jonathan Lovejoy

ℰLIZABETHAN

or

"The Assemblies"

Volume XII

Jonathan Lovejoy

Such is the grandest music among us—

Poets…

Such are the wildest thoughts among us—

Composers…

The Book of Raven

367th Assembly

1612

A comet in the sky—

Will precede the Second Coming—

A feathery tail of light

Up in the night sky

No need for panic—

No story to tell.

Hell.

1613

Open your heart to Him, Mr. Goodlife—

Your life and your soul

Are mortgaged to the hilt.

When the bill comes due—

You can't pay it

It was paid in full—

By Christ Jesus on the Cross.

1614

I wrote a poem when I was six
It sang a happy tune
A song called "The Ghostly Armour"
A verse I wrote in June--

A suit of armour walked the halls
I did not run and hide--
But when it stopped to look at me-
I saw no one inside!

Put on the whole armour of God
Since now that I am grown
So I can walk my journey through
This wilderness alone

368th Assembly

1615

*Y*ou've been answering all the same questions--
Answerlessy.
The prairie girl scolds the picnic—
Mercilessly.

Wisdom under the prairie tree—
Smiling.

1616

*T*he North tweeters a phone call—

With new business to say

Get ready for a smoking gun—

Its called "The Passion Play"

1617

The Dragon sees with eyes that stare
On the eve of Eschatology—
The Age of the rainbow is ended—
When fire falls from the sky

No city since the dawn of time
Hath seen such fearful sights
When the Moon turns to darkness
In a nighttime sky

1618

And when the wind blew in, the gorilla caught him—
In jungle forest leaves
Madness bestowed upon the earth—
Its time to harvest the sheaves

Bringing in the sheaves—
Bringing in the sheaves—
Satan comes rejoicing—
Bringing in the sheaves

Child *molestation* is a sign
Of time turning the eaves
When Satan comes rejoicing—
Bringing in the sheaves

Evil as was never seen
And none truly believes—
Child *molestation* is a sign
Turning toward the Eaves—

Pack your bags and look up—
Before the Messiah leaves
Satan will come rejoicing—
Bringing in the sheaves

Child *molestation* is the sign
That no one truly grieves
When Satan comes rejoicing—
Bringing in the sheaves

Mothers sleep with teenage boys—
And wear it on their sleeves
Fathers sleep with little girls
And hide it in their sleeves

Child *molestation* is the sign
That none truly receives—
As Satan comes rejoicing
Bringing in the sheaves

369th Assembly

Jonathan Lovejoy

1619

Symbols return a dreadful rain—

To burn a soul to ruin

Revised wandering comes to naught

On the eve of pain again

1620

Angelinari rises up
For the Coletti pen
To carry melodies aloft
And back to earth again

Concertos for full orchestra
And every sound within
Sings a song of sixpence to me—
So I'll remember when

Music such as was never heard
In modern day nor then
Antonio Amadeus by—
Angelinari's pen

1621

Muse whispers a melody
To the composer's ear
As well too--the lonely poet
Until a song is clear

Neither mountain view nor sunset
Nor ocean in the spring
Can inspire as a melody—
By Muse's golden wing

Melodies for heaven to hear—
And for the earth to sing
Touched on the poet's violin—
A pen and paper string

1622

The spirit of death tonight
Displays a gallery in the fog
Illuminated by the lamplights—
Children of the Lonely

Roaming the streets unaware
Of what dangers lurk the night road—
Crickets chirping their demise—
On the streets of this town

Wayward sons in the dead of night—
Pray, come home again!

Jonathan Lovejoy

370th Assembly

1623

I wrote an opera for free—
Those that promised to pay
Never told of the money due—
So I would go away

But there should be compensation—
For the death of a soul
The burial of hopes and dreams—
For a goal unfulfilled

The money they promised was gone—
My Opera was for free!
The man in charge would not discuss—
The evil done to m

1624

Untie and lower me—

That I may sleep in the ground

Give my life to another—

Let me go to Heaven

Dead horses do not respond—

To beating

There's no need—

So let sleeping horses lie

Untie and lower me—

That I may sleep in the ground

Let others have—

What I have never seen

Answered prayers—

Hope fulfilled

Joy—

Prosperity.

Jonathan Lovejoy

Untie and lower me
That I may sleep in the ground
Give my life to another—
Let me go to Heaven.

1625

Coletti rises up again—

To claim her rightful pen

Angelinari is buried—

In her coffin by the sea

Coletti composes a song—

A symphony in G

To mourn the death of melody

In her coffin by the sea

Carmen Angelina Coletti

Born on a minor key—

To play the Truth until she sleeps—

In her coffin by the sea.

1626

Down the road of life

Go many twists and turns—

Detours--and roadblocks—

Obstacles along the way

But on the open road

There is a smooth ride forward—

From one point of nothing

To the next

Birds sing—

Thieves thief—

Or rather, robbers steal—

If you may

Storytellers story

Poets poet

Novelists novel away

The road ahead crumbles and falls

From here to eternity

Until there is nowhere left to travel

Elizabethan XII

Nothing to steal—
Nothing to sing—
Nothing to talk upon—

Nothing to write

371st Assembly

1627

The phone tweeters my demise—
Go ahead and die!

Stop beating a dead horse—your life
Then die and go to Hell!

You're not going to Heaven, you bum!
You're a worthless piece of nothing!

Trash fell from the sky when you were born—
So go ahead and die!

A fool—with so little talent
You couldn't see success with a hundred eyes—

Your father and your mother both despised you
So do the world a favor—

Go ahead and die!

Take the pills and be done with it—
Garbage falls to you from the sky

Jonathan Lovejoy

Why do you persist—insist on living
Do yourself a favor—

Go ahead and die!

Your legacy is fecal and blood—
So go ahead and die!

1628

Sunshine and purple flowers—

What more is there to gain?

Except a man be born again—

Cloudy skies and rain

1629

He circled the barn in a speed wagon—
Though why, I couldn't tell
Then his life was touched by Heaven
While mine was touched by Hell

Wickedness and Evil prosper
Every day and night
While Goodness dances a tango—
With Poverty and Blight

1630

I wish I could breathe free—
Like the birds in the trees
Who laugh a song when they see me—
Longing to be free

With no weight to carry—
No burden in my soul
No walls and no windows—
Closing in on me

What sin is it to beg Him—
Hasten eternal sleep?
Where I can rest—
With the birds in the trees—

Joyful to be free

Jonathan Lovejoy

372nd Assembly

1631

Veins carry a message in blue—

Your life is a playground

When they complement your letter—

Do be wary of them

1632

*L*isten to the man of music—

For Carmen Coletti

Let her carry the name chosen

Through perpetuity—

Every major and minor key

Plays ingenuity—

She proclaims the word of the Lord—

Anointed destiny

1633

I can feel freedom calling—
Like a gust of wind
An echo from the future
Forward—and back again

A cool breeze
On a warm summer's day—
Cannot compare to it

1634

The reign of the spider ended—
Hallelujah to the Lamb!
Victory over Lucifer—
On the morning of his demise

The path to the Throne is unobscured—
By Satan in the wise
Under gray skies, the barrier falls—
By a promise from on high

Jonathan Lovejoy

373rd Assembly

1635

Yellow and orange—the fruit of life

Corrupted in the river

Problems unknown—rising

On the road to freedom

1636

Dear Heavenly father—

Send a cool breeze

To warm my heart to thee

By the Summer Wind—

In days of the desert moon

Send thy cooling touch to me

Soothe the burning—which remains—

Bygone curses—

From the Land of Rain

High over the birds that fly

I see the Prince of the Power of the Air

As a cloud in the sky—

Beneath thy Throne

Fearful of the Promise—

Thy cooling breeze—

The blessing bestowed from thee

1637

Rocking through the bad luck

A white horse on Red Rock Rails

Casper's eye—

In mocking tone—

Watching the greedy fool die

Pride goeth before destruction

A haughty spirit before a fall—

Ride the Red Rock Rails of Greed—

Be a fool and die!

1638

White marble statues look on
Right before my eyes
The turning blade is cut off—
In confiscated power

The metal clangs—*Clang!*
It hits a statue in the mouth
To twist it to oblivion

The bull head statue becomes a man
And turns to where I stand
Knowing again—that the eggs are broken—
With no rain upon the farm

Jonathan Lovejoy

374th Assembly

1639

Green and purple carry the message—

On the wardrobe of perpetuity

In the house of poverty, the ancestry strives—

To live above the dirt

1640

"*T*ell your husband to keep writing"—
Another lie in gold
To perpetuate the delusion
Until his mind is gone

None of your samples are any good
You won't make it above the line—
A born loser never quits—
And is never shown the way

The ancestry in glowing red—
"They'll never let you in
Because I'll see to it myself—
That you will never win"

1641

The grass over the prairie green
Is blowing in the wind—
Beneath a drowning, fervent rain
Forewarning of the end

The rain over the prairie green
Is blowing in the wind—
Lightning! Illuminate the waves!
Forewarning of the end

The tree over the prairie green
Is blowing in the wind
Beneath the crowning Voice of God—
Forewarning of the end

1642

Cruising the amaranthine isle

For ingenuity

In hopeful knowledge where it lies—

Though it has gone away

The flag doth wave behind the Cross—

In manmade tradition

Is John Mark Karr's extradition

A sign of where we're in?

Pack up, look up—we're going up!

I heard the preacher say

Perhaps even in our lifetime—

The final Judgment Day

Jonathan Lovejoy

375th Assembly

Jonathan Lovejoy

1643

Sanity's light is so bright
I cannot endure it—
Take me back to the shadows—
Where Delusion and Insanity live

Where spirits gather and whisper lies—
False hopes for a better life
Where the warm sunlight of Clarity is darkened
By a cloud of confusion

Dreams and visions are wishes and fears
Perpetuated as Truth
When in reality they are nothing—
But images to ignore

1644

The unicorn runs into the forest—
To whereabouts unseen
To hide away the white magic
As though it had never been

Although the white witch knows the truth—
She is forbidden to say—
The meaning of the graveyard trip
Unkindly fades away

"You're going in circles," Sylvia says
Something in your life is dead—
Upon the sofa of lost dreams
With Truth inside my head

1645

*C*ruising along the road of life—

In the beauty of creation

Saturn inspires admiration

As we arrive the motel station

Admiring a lost place in life

At the stop on the road to nowhere

Told by the spirit *"Fetch the food—*

You've got nothing more for which to care"

1646

Before the birth of melody

When the serpent is dead

Three stand ready for their labour--

Apart from fear and dread

Offices of Prosperity

A future fountain pool—

Green leaves burdened by God to grow—

Under the Golden Rule

Jonathan Lovejoy

376th Assembly

Jonathan Lovejoy

1647

In the Supermarket of Death—
I see hopelessness for sale
Turn thy head upon thy shoulders—
And see which way to go

Inside the market of lost dreams—
I see Death for sale
For a life that has come to nothing—
For a life that was lived in vain

1648

Angels and demons! Come and see!
When Faith touches humanity
Unique in God's creation—are we!

Angels and demons, now take heed—
Growth from the grain of mustard seed—
With permission to procede!

1649

Build a house around a tree—

Then bide your time, patiently

1650

Generations will know it as—

The Farm Girl's Opera

Genius clipped from the Barber shop

On the streets of Seville

A lightning bolt of melody

Flashed of angelic skill

In the Twelve Days of Rossini—

A prophecy fulfilled

Now Coletti carries a tune

Third in the Trilogy

The Crown Prince—The Guilty Mother—

The end of History

Jonathan Lovejoy

377th Assembly

Jonathan Lovejoy

1651

On the shores of insanity
You've lost touch with reality
Piddling a middling and tittling
While the sand erodes away

Torn down, brick by brick
Your castle by the sea
Washed away by the surf
Inevitably

1652

Take a trip to one year ago—
To see what it is you know
Look at the Lawn of White Sand
That grew the patches of green

1653

*W*ill you forgive me, Miss Mary—

For all the things I've done?

Cancel thine hatred for me!

1654

The blue team gathers for battle—
Young souls—ready for death
To play in the Autumn Wind
Under Friday night lights again

The white team takes a steady breath—
In preparation to die

1655

*I*n the high rise of lost hope—
Down the halls of poverty
Despair claims a road to success
In hopeless desperation

False hope plays a chicken bone
In dead expectation
Unable to see the Sea of Graves—
In haunting memory

Despair leads to the Wall of Treats
Promising to know
Being unable to give it a go—
In the show predestined to fail

378th Assembly

Jonathan Lovejoy

1656

The maestro did not find the tune

For the Katie Flower

No genius and diversity—

For the Lady's Hour

From the Carmen Coletti pen

The Earth would turn again—

Inspiration for the last days—

And the Twilight of Sin

The Players of Orchestra's Light

Would know the melody

On the second coming of Christ—

And eschatology

1657

Desperate housewives on TV—
From sea to shining sea
Hobble around with the Terri Bird—
In good natured ambiguity

The Godspear has a curse to bear—
Branded in his name
A burning rash upon his soul
And his spirit just the same

1658

The crowd will break your heart today—
But then they'll never go away
Find it in your mind to say—
"I wish they wouldn't stay"

Guard your heart against them—
There's a price they're willing to pay
To see you broken and bleeding Death—
Pretending to be okay

1659

Eros is short for erosion—
The end of wedded bliss
When young love turn to corosion
Poisoning the kiss—

"You arrogant son-of-a-bitch"
She argues quietly—
"You can keep the women chasing you—
Too stupid to know the deal"

"I don't want you anyway, bitch"
He argues quietly—
The rumblings of an explosion
At Amberlane next door

Jonathan Lovejoy

379th Assembly

1660

If she had been over there screaming—
City hall would fall
Big beautiful blue eyes
Above a bouncing, bubbling bosom

Raw meat tells the story
Of unfinished business
Lurking the complex of dead dreams—
Feeding delusion

Eros wobbles the wigwam
Of beauty and the breasts
Reminders of the Agony of Want—
And Desire unfulfilled

1661

Keisha New England loves me—
Truth dying in the rain
Her heart broken by the new Rule—
Which took her away from me

Old friends and the red gun
Appearing in the rain
Hop along age without wisdom—
Burdened by the pain

Memories of two kisses fade—
Dying in the rain

1662

Black feathers burned into the page—
On the letter of life
Indications of a future
Burdened by the raven

Against divinely appointed evil—
There is no victory
A lifetime of prayer and hope
Will end in utter defeat

Although it will be sad—
Accept the Death of Melody
Bury her inside a tomb
So heaven and earth can rest

1663

There are prices to pay

Crosses to bear

Comeuppances that are overdue

When you have parted the Red Sea

Don't cry,

Don't ask why—

When He tells you to speak to the rock

But you strike it in anger

And you will not see the Promised Land

When you have written and played—

The greatest piano concertos of all time

Don't cry

Don't asky why—

When you wake up in the middle of the night

Aged 35

Poisoned—

Broke—

Dead

Jonathan Lovejoy

When you have written in 12 days
The greatest comic opera ever heard—
Whereupon demand, The Paris Opera—
The greatest overture of all time—
Don't cry
Don't ask why
When disease and fear overtake—
When every critic despises—
For the rest of your days

There are prices to pay
Crosses to bear
Comeuppances that are overdue

When your mind is a rose garden
Where every verse is grown
Genius like a bouquet gathered
Don't cry—
Don't ask why—
When you are a prisoner of your Homestead
And every flower you send
Is clipped—
Unwatered.
Ridiculed
Until you lie in the coffin
And the flowers you have gathered
Are nurtured over your grave—

And the graves of all those who laughed you to sickness

Tears—

And Death

Jonathan Lovejoy

380th Assembly

Jonathan Lovejoy

1664

On the road to Prosperity

The Lauderdale abandons me
As I struggle for what I can—
To reach the golden sand

The ancestry plays a record
From Perpetuity
The same old song of Poverty—
And Incongruity

With knowledge of trouble brewing
Down the road to new life—
Another opportunity is lost—
Unavoidably

1665

Start the engine and press the gas—

Toward your destiny—
Blackbird dreams and visions—go!
Back from where you came

Commerce and invitations fly
In the dark of night
Memories of days gone by
On our fateful flight—

The saddest truth that can be known
Concerning history
Is that every choice is already made—
By Predestiny

1666

*T*he queen says, *"God can dream a bigger dream—*

Than we can dream for ourselves—"

But unearned suffering

Is not redemptive in this life

The cemetery tells the tale

Each grave stone speaks the truth—

Forty years of hard labour

Dreaming a little dream—

Cancer in retirement

A poverty coffin bed

God dreams a bigger dream

Than we can dream for ourselves—

A bigger dream of pain and suffering—

And death

1667

I see Death walking to where I am—
From far across the field
A place where prosperity grew
'Til it was killed by Him

Death strolls across the barren field
Slowly to where I stand

1668

Along the timeline, there are three
And yet these three are one
Mozart, Rossini, Coletti
Chosen under the Sun

The ancestry speaks from prison
On the Sunday morning
Engaged by manmade religion—
Piety adorning

Pray the demons away tonight
Until the deed is done—
The Father, Son, and Holy Ghost—
And yet these three are one

381st Assembly

1669

$\mathcal{L}$ord JESUS—

I believe you died on the Cross for my sins

Come into my heart—

And save my soul.

Amen

1670

A farmer walked into the room
To tell me he was dead
He had a black face with no eyes
A hat was on his head—

Go back into the fields, I said—
And leave me to my bed.

1671

A zephyr rolls the prairie blue
An unfamiliar wind--
Blue skies descend a whirlwind
To accentuate the trend

The tendency of this life for trouble--
Never seems to end.

1672

An untasty poverty meal
From the deep blue sea
Leaves "The Passion" author disconcerted—
On the eve of tragedy

But in the realm of darkness
Where the ancestry waits
Displays a gift beyond measure
An unearthly treasure

The colors of the Trinity
Adorn the purple sea
One place of hope in darkness
And total despair

382nd Assembly

1673

We gathered round the great big ball

No spinning energy

Too gigantic for Christmastime

Made only to inspire

A gift of uncommon beauty

For your heart's desire

1674

Such an incredible decision—
You have to make for yourself
Do it with precision—
And an epic vision

Because no one is going to help you—
Rather, derision will litter your path
Like confetti—
Or the petals of a yellow rose

Your work requires revision—
Beyond what you can know

1675

The farmer sat on a coffin—
Then he spat on a grave
In the place I had walked upon—
That housed the life I gave

You have to memorize the Psalm—
Your harvest yield to save

383rd Assembly

1676

The argument with the ancestry—
Burns no blue and black fire
As we endeavor to bitterness
With no flame of desire

Outside the house of dreams—
As the sky turns to night
The white sand grows the harvest—
Waiting to be born

Beauty rides the chariot by—
Nearby the evening
Immodesty in innocence
For purposes unknown

The farmer speaks of scriptures
In turning from the day
Showing me where the dead is buried—
And corrupted away

1677

Throw a signal to the bypass
In the drowning rain—
On our stroll beside the river wide
To hear the rest of the tale

On the outer edges of insanity
Waiting to be born
The answer lies intestate
In the field of grain

Moving, waving, flowing in the breeze
With future lives to gain
The answer lies intestate—
Drowning in the rain

1678

The truth speaks with clarity
So one can understand
Honor your chosen path in life—
And all it may demand

Look toward Heaven, now and then
For a helping hand

1679

And people say, "there is no God"—

What is flight, then—

If not a miracle

The whirling of a breeze

The screaming of a wind

And then, we are carried aloft—

To make light of every bird—

In flight

Jonathan Lovejoy

384th Assembly

Jonathan Lovejoy

1680

Cruising the highway of dead dreams
Under a phantom night
The egg floats harmlessly above—
The Williams and Lookinland Knight

When the woman seeks the municipality—
No help she receives
Help of this kind comes only from God
To him who truly believes

Reed accepts no piano keys—
In the house of perfection
Circumspection begs to choke—
The road to prosperity

1681

To slay the Gorgon Medusa
The writhing serpent head—
Pray, deliver thine sword of Truth
On her neck until dead

Then take no look into her eyes
The tide of fear and dread
Thy bone and body turned to stone
A statue-coffin bed

1682

*T*he lights are out in Perpetuity—

At the storefront of shadows

Where lost dreams go to die

Again and again

Heffernan delivers a message

To the Rain Wanderer

A barrier to life and freedom—

Is your chosen path

1683

The top of the grassy field is white
When blowing in the wind—
Each stalk gives their melodies play
In harmony with ease

Music and messages in the grass
Flowing beneath the trees
Chimes from Eden to Armageddon
In Gethsemane's Reprise

Waves upon the Sea of Grass
In days beyond the Bee
Keys of Salvation from above—
The Sea of Galilee

Jonathan Lovejoy

385th Assembly

1684

Every now and then

I see the wind—

It flows with purpose—

Everywhere it goes

And everywhere I've been

Through the grassy field—

To where I rest

Waiting to get in

I knock on the doors of Faith and Hope—

Will they let me in?

1685

What is a rocking chair

But an upright bed—

With no cushion—

And no lid

Open thine eyes—quickly!

To see that the bed is upright

With no cushion—

And no lid

1686

What my career has amounted—

Nightmares and rejection

Every night—another vision

Purposeful dejection

1687

A longtime swings the dance floor
And swing time Hallelujah!
Aliens unplug the ancestry—
From rationality

Irrational assumptions
Reveal the heart—
And the soul of perversion
Rather let the timeline flow undisturbed—
Until the aliens are gone

Parents along the timeline
Are alien half the time
Improper motivations bestowed—
In bitter regret

386th Assembly

1688

The farmer is an angry sort

With interference to report--

His retort was—*"They saw crops in my field"*

But they decide to cut anyway

Intruders in the cropfield

For remuneration and sport

1689

Demons, ineffectual—

Knocking at my door
I see one through the window—
Craving to come in

The loud-mouthed bully seeks me out
The white witch falls—and breaks the lamp
The house is raised on lumber sticks
At the clearing in the Woods

Where the demons parade in and out
I rest my sleeping bed
Just jump the grave and shut your mouth—
Everything you've done is dead

1690

That's where we found the bodies

That's where we started looking

Gather them up in a pile—

So we can bury them

Step away from the gravesight

And claim your life again

Knock on the doors Ad Nauseum—

Until they let you in

!

1691

The first leaf was bit by autumn
In the flowering tree today
What poison killed its summer green—
But let the others stay?

When the leaf was bit by autumn—
It withered and died away

387th Assembly

1692

Generations along the line
In the Office of No Direction
Burdened by lifetimes of pain—
And certain imperfection

When the burden of 1000 miles—
Is multiplied by ten
Look to Heaven and walk alone—
By the power of God within.

1693

At first, there is the feat of clay—
In sorrow will her beauty lay.
At last, her scars show every sin—
In Judgement, will the evil win.

1694

The iron spider ends the trip

Of such, one cannot give the slip

Problems too permanent to clip—

In Perpetuity

Crumbled roads—open graves

Horizon trees too dead to save

An unsolved mystery He gave—

From Now to Infinity

1695

Delusion given in my dreams—

To torment my heart to ruin

388th Assembly

1696

*T*ain't nothing to Jacob's Liar

He gave him that hat to wear—

A white hat with no brim

On a whim dropped from the air

A good harp moved over the concerto

When the blue hat moved across the sky

Answers lie in the jet plane

Blazing the night sky

1697

*A*good harp moved over the concerto

When the blue hat moved across the sky

Answers lie in the jet plane

Blazing the night sky

1698

Jon Benet Ramsey on my lap
Nursing an ankle sprain
In days before the little girl—
Went drifting in the rain

Her memory is a gravestone—
Her loving heart in vain
In days after the little girl—
Went drifting in the rain

Her life and her death are a sign—
Sent to a world in pain
Remember when the little girl—
Went drifting in the rain

1699

Pick the Armageddon Flower

Before your busride to nowhere

Decide on your final hour

As the dream dies

Satan loves the death of a dream

The end of insanity

When a person realizes what he is—

Accursed humanity

389th Assembly

1700

When I look in the mirror

I see the curse of God—

Looking back at me.

1701

With the top of my head sawed off—

I act like half a brain

With the top of my head sawed off—

My brain drain maintains a pain

Adrift on a sea of hopelessness—

Drowning in the rain

Angelina Jolie—

Watches empty ideas on the plain

When the top of my head gets sawed off—

And my life is cut in twain

1702

Passengers on board the night train

Are deluded to be sure

Riding the train in a false hope—

But knowing just the same—

Cruising to their destination

Which is Death

1703

Looking for the genius cloth

In the pile of mediocrity

Hearing the voice of inspiration

Somewhere in the weave

While the ancestry looks on

The genius cloth is found

390th Assembly

1704

The train arrives its rendezvous

Which is the grassy ground

Riders step into the night

To find their burial mound

Strolling the grassy field

Darkness all around

1705

*C*ondescention and Patronization

Are in the water

Drink it—

And you will become indoctrinated—

Intoxicated.

1706

*T*hose who claim to know Christianity—

Don't know everything

Because Knowledge is Faith—

Faith in Heaven is one side

When the Messiah comes

But faith in the other side—

Is Hell—

To them who don't believe.

1707

A man was pulled into a fan
And ground into a mess
In a manufacturing plant—
Where safety is the plan

Though he was dead before it was done—
They were doing what they can
To stop his body from being ground—
In the blade of the giant fan

We saw it happen on TV—
When the man died in the fan

391st Assembly

1708

The blue bug flies the autumn day
The color of the sky
At the white pane kitchen window
The prairie green nearby

1709

The ancestry says, *close your mouth*

And listen to the wind

Major problems are still crawling—

Before the job is done

Poverty beckons from the past

To hail a job undone

Jonathan Lovejoy

1710

The bus to Perpetuity—

Rolls down Williamston Road

To reveal the pain of excess

And Failure's agony

The skies over my hometown

Are colored as the sea

But covered by a mass of gray

And reclusivity

1711

With two demons in our kitchen
How goes the food?
The two of them stand seven feet—
Taking our food.

Two obstacles along our path
Killing our mood
Filling their bags from the cupboards—
To kill our mood.

Pray the two demons from our home—
Or come unglued.
We defeat principalities—
Or come unglued.

392nd Assembly

1712

Follow the arrows down the road

Regardless where they lead

The green arrows appear in space—

To satisfy your need

Though you can't know where they will go

Follow them, indeed

1713

The pain I live shall be buried—

When my body is gone

It will be interred with the dust

Under the prairie lawn

1714

Go to the bedroom—

Go for your carnal repose

Lust hath conceived?

To bring forth sin?

Heaven only knows!

Jonathan Lovejoy

393rd Assembly

Jonathan Lovejoy

1715

The red river runs the white plain

In days before the autumn rain

Colored by those who lived and died—

And those that still remain

1716

The moutain peak lies just ahead

Above my weary head

Dreading what climb is left to do—

Before I rest my head

Shall I bed beneath the mountain earth—

Or the prairie land instead?

1717

On the road to immortality
These are the signs I see
Pointing the way to Poverty—
Or Prosperity—

John Denver. Oprah Winfrey
And Stephen King I see
Hilary Clinton, Maya Angelou
Bruce Lee and The Black Eyed Peas

Martin Luther King, Jesus Christ
And Abraham Lincoln are three

Randall Cunningham and Warren Moon
Bob Costas and Culture Club
Michael Jackson, Lionel Richie, Madonna
And Megan Mullally agree

On the road to immortality
These are the signs I see—

Elizabethan XII

Jack and Rexella Van Impe
Gayle King, Conan O' Brian
Renee Zellweger, Faith Ford
And Steven Spielberg decree

Kelly Ripa, Ann Curry
Demond Wilson, Redd Foxx
Ray Charles, Fifty Cent
And Emily Dickinson for me

Jude Law, Robert Deniro
Flavor Flav, Brett Favre
Katie Couric, John Lennon
And Paul McCartney for tea

Gioacchino Rossini and John Williams
Chris Tucker, Steve Young
Joe Montana, Terri Hatcher
And Carol O'Conner to be

John Amos, Richard Pryor
Ann B. Davis and Robert Reed
Barry Williams, Christopher Knight
And Mike Lookinland memory

Mel Gibson and Kevin James
Regis Philbin, Sylvester Stallone
Along with every road sign I see—
Is Angelina Jolie

Jonathan Lovejoy

On the road to immortality—
These are the signs I see
Showing me the way to Poverty—
And Eschatology

1718

Hear the warnings in the wind--

A dream is coming to an end

Get in the machine--wash it clean

Free yourself from the prison you're in

Jonathan Lovejoy

394th Assembly

1719

The progeny looks on—

At the backward fool's endeavor

Having no more strength for battle

Knowing only pain

1720

*W*here do dreams go to die?

What world are they in?

The earth mourns the death of a dream

The breaking of a heart

Jonathan Lovejoy

1721

The violent color carries a song—

Where strings punctuate a rhythm

Hailing from Raleigh, North Carolina

The sign of the second coming

A man must identify—

And obey his calling

Then its back to life, the song says—

Back to reality

1722

Feline treachery in white

Flying around the room—

Like bad luck risen from the grave—

In a prophecy of doom

1723

A cheap belt is fit for the trash—

Though someone will wear it

Those burdened by ignorance

Or poverty

In the Office of Dead Dreams—

Throw the cheap belt away

Elizabethan XII

395th Assembly

1724

When I see the coffin tonight—

I'll know my plight is done
The burden of life will cast off
As Death and I are one

Is it really over?
Or only just begun?

1725

Satan smiled when the lady died
When the children of the lady's family cried—
A gust of wind came—
Then it blew the lady from the balcony

Her body tumbled and twirled through space
From her balcony hiding place
There was laughter at the burial
When their grief could not subside

Mother's body lay in the ground
By a gust of wind—she died

1726

The material girl locks the door

Refusing to let me in

Through feeble power, I make it through—

To the second door, and then

The third, fourth and fifth door—

Over and over again

Jonathan Lovejoy

1727

Earthquakes gathered across the globe

Quaking red lines on the map

The chances to life and freedom

Are slim to none

396th Assembly

1728

The lady strolls in confidence

Down the streets of ill repute

In front of the no tell motel

And the Pink Rind

1729

Although every demon in hell

Has been dispatched to me

Shall I give up the fight to win

Or on to Victory?

The road is dark and treacherous

On my journey to be free

Asking help from above

Receiving only misery

Jonathan Lovejoy

1730

The most divinely inspired poet—
In the history of mankind
Is the Queen of Wicked Verse
Letters unfettered to bind

The heart and soul of a mortal
Under a divine decree
To sail the winds of melancholy
Across a lonely sea

1731

$\mathcal{D}$o women have rows done to them—

Or do they have a place to row?

1732

The little girl sees Mrs. Denton on the sofa

She takes Mrs. Denton's hand

The little girl is crazy—

Because there is no one on the sofa.

Mrs. Denton died last Saturday from a stroke.

The little girl sees Mr. Denton too—

The little girl is crazy—

He died of a heart attack two years ago.

But while she holds hands with the air—

She insists that they are there.

In the chair.

397th Assembly

Jonathan Lovejoy

1733

Spring can be a means to control—

Summer is here to stay

Autumn rolls by and by

Winter is on the way

1734

Riding down hope street
These are the people we meet—
Failure, Despair, and Poverty
Haunting the road

Due to experience—
I stop.
At the bottom of the hill—
Knowing that the road is flooded
And all my dreams are killed.

1735

No wind upon the sea—
Still.
No breeze over the prairie green—
Still.

No breath over top the grasses wave
No storm at this horizon
Tranquil.
Under the Harvest Moon—

Not joy—but peace
A prophecy of calm
Fulfilled.

Over the windowsill—
An echo—of what winds may blow—
No wind upon the sea
No breeze over the prairie green

1736

Lift the house and watch it crumble—

Power and pieces intertwined

What deadliness crawls up from the rubble

With malice, malevolence and malign

Jonathan Lovejoy

398th Assembly

Jonathan Lovejoy

1737

Coins register the fountain—

Of pain and agony

In the burdening time of the sweet drink—

At the edge of algidity

Coins shine the symbol

Of missed opportunity

Of which there will be more than plenty—

At the grocery station

Never again will a day go by

Unfilled with regret—

The sorrow and the pain of living

Is too heavy to bear

1738

Of two that are one and the same—

Insanity and Grief

The pain of grief alters the mind

Robbing it—like a thief.

A grieving soul is a drunkard

Aboard Agony's Wine

With access to the blocks of light

Awake--ye muses nine!

Seeing those sights best left unseen

Born of women and men

Crushed by the solemn weight of life—

And ground to dust by sin

Jonathan Lovejoy

1739

Open your heart to Divinity—
Let it become part of thee
A window unto him is Art—
And Creativity

Handel's oratorio—
Mozart's piano key
Rossini's laughing woodwinds—
Beethoven's symphony

See him in the bars of music!
Hear his divine decree:
Seek ye first the Kingdom of God—
And draw near unto me

1740

Seventeen seventy six—
The beginning of the end
Signed to life on July 4th—
Let the final days begin!

The sky above the world has darkened—
To unseeing eyes
Horrors too terrible to know
In latter day disguise

Awaiting the voice of thunder
To rain lightning to the ground
By Principalities and Powers—
Wickedness shall abound

399th Assembly

1741

Prepare the harvest of sweet corn—

Despite the prophecy forlorn

A living death—foretold

Too far along the timeline to hold her

The weight of Atlas on my shoulder

Grief from days of old

By the Harvest Moon—the field of grain

Gathered in the Autumn Rain

Alone and in the cold

1742

Be careful on your night trip

Lest you give yourself the slip

Unseen treachery—

Waiting—

Underneath your feet.

Be careful on your night trip

Watch it when you slip

Lest you find yourself a broken neck—

Hiding underneath a step—

Somewhere along your clip.

1743

Line all your ducks up in a row—
Then, its lickety split!
Accept the challenge shown to you—
Be sure to never quit

Failure is just a stepping stone
Toward what you need to get
To rectify a life of pain—
And ashen gray regret

Line the baby chicks in a row!
Complete the task at hand—
Knowledge and Wisdom perservere—
To live what God has planned

Jonathan Lovejoy

1744

Remember what the scriptures say
In order to get along
Neither is the race for the swift—
Nor is it for the strong

The Tree of Life blows in the wind—
To whisper right from wrong

1745

Brave students enter class in lies—
And modern day deceit
The Ancestry gets a new dog
Old friends have come and gone

In the gloom of the evening day
There's panic on the way
Concerning a task left undone—
A price still left to pay

400th Assembly

1746

*T*hey say—*you might as well let go*

They'll never let you in

But the truth is—if you don't fight

How can you ever win?

1747

She struck the first piano key—

I knew I was in love

Without a doubt—she makes me see

Happiness from above

1748

Metaphor is easy—Clarity is hard

One is a mountain snowflake

The Other—

A drop of desert rain.

Jonathan Lovejoy

1749

The anointing cannot stay hidden

A bushel glows from within

A light that shines in darkness

To guide the hearts of men

401st Assembly

Jonathan Lovejoy

1750

Bad luck plagues the weary traveler

On their trip to the Promised Land—

Feline eyes of misfortune—

And ordained treachery

Some who leave captivity

Will die along the way

But still destined for the Exodus—

And a skeleton in the clay

1751

The Autumn grass whispers an "S" wave
Spectacular in the breeze
White waves—whish the grassy sea of green
On the eve of the Hayfield Harvest Queen

To gather the browning prairie—
She plucks the waving grasses clean
When her messages prophecy the "S" wave—
The Autumn Bluebird is seen

Jonathan Lovejoy

1752

*A*cknowledge the four leaf clover
Take heed to its design
Sketch its shade in the border right
Or you'll be left behind

Its not Perserverance, Luck or Skill—
But Fate that guides the mind

402nd Assembly

Jonathan Lovejoy

1753

A feathered cow in the meadow—

Underneath the willow tree

Set to take flight like a hawk

To come and devour me

1754

Emily spoke discreetly—

As she clipped the garden weed—

Success is counted sweetest—

By those who ne'er succeed

A flower from her garden

Of ingenuities

Jonathan Lovejoy

1755

*T*he sign of the Cross—

Is burned into history

From the shores of 1611

To the 21st century

Seek not a divine calling

It will find you instead

The burden of it is from Calvary

The shape of the accursed tree

The Flame of Responsibility

Seeks the soul of Destiny—

To burn on it the sign of the Cross—

A divine legacy

1756

Stay at the foot of the Cross—
When Judgment is raining down
Better to die in Salvation
Than to live in world renown

Kiss the wood of the accursed tree
Touch it as you should
Taste the blood of the Chosen One
Rained into the wood

Ingrained into the soul of man
Is the order of what we should
Which is to touch the foot of the Cross—
Where our Lord and Savior died

Jonathan Lovejoy

403rd Assembly

Jonathan Lovejoy

1757

Strolling through the Autumn Field

Beneath the forest trees

Souls united in funtime

In the crashing waves of wind

The view from above is sin—

Let the autumn feast begin!

1758

Outside in the cold rain—

Dreariness deserves a day in the sun

Shock! Appearing on my face—

I hear a demon in the fireplace!

My heart quickens a pace!

The demon calls me from the fireplace!

1759

Attend to the task at hand—
Obey the master plan
Call the fumigation man
Its time to take a stand

Ride through the empty streets
Still burdened by the night
Smash your way along the flight
Engage those who wish to fight

Take a ride with the fat man—
Go with him while you can
Stay in tune with the master plan
Attend to the task at hand

1760

Look forward to the completion—
Of the unknown journey
Gauge a point at the horizon
Then walk until you're free

What does it matter of Failure—
When the trip is done
It was a road you were destined to take
A mountain by Fate to climb—

When the journey comes to an end
Remember the angel's chime
You could not have escaped this trip--
Through the Winds of Time

Jonathan Lovejoy

404th Assembly

Jonathan Lovejoy

1761

I saw a rider in the field—

No regard for the harvest yield

From afar, the farmer rides in—

With yet to see the scar.

1762

There are those who skip through life on a rose petal carpet.

Moving effortlessly across the years by privileges—

The advantages afforded by birth.

Through no fault of their own--they go from one point of happiness to the next--

With the dim, sedated look of complacency in their eyes.

The joy of life over contented expressions.

Every so often, the rose path knows a space of loneliness—and heartache,

And they bewail to the heavens about the little sorrow.

A few hours, a few days of sadness is an eternity,

Even causing regret for times of origin.

But they soon reach the next point of happiness,

And forget this brief sorrow and misery.

But for some, *birth* begins the Lonely Season—

And these soon discover a path littered with thistles,

While they move—painfully—from one point of suffering to the next.

And they might travel across all the years to their graves,

Without ever realizing the hardest part of the truth—

The most horrific portion of the Truth—

That the greater part of their suffering was caused—
By other people.

1763

The new world preacher loves money—

The agony of debt

Making others err from the Faith

And suffer in regret

1764

I was a cake t'was never baked
Promises unbroken
Lies born—from truth never spoken
Causing a heart to break

Her name appeared in blocks of light
Grieving a soul to ache

405th Assembly

Jonathan Lovejoy

1765

The illness reaches far and wide—
On the eve of destruction
The mob boss says—*you've got 'ms'*
The king says—*success will never be.*

1766

Trained by houses gone by—

The sunlight focused on its enemies

The prescription is Failure—

In the evening day

1767

Kept him from being a downy weaver

It was all a light

Warrants clean and touch my skin—

Ready for a fight

1768

Concerning pie in the sky—

Do lick the platter clean
Until the day you die—
Concrete footsteps don't matter

406th Assembly

1769

All your labour was for nought

Chicken and turkey on the grill

My time with this dance parter—

Is about to lose its thrill

1770

Two bluebirds in the yard
In the autumn day
Visited by a redbird—
Inviting them to play

1771

The bluebird sings an elegy—

Beneath the clouds of heaven

Death is the cricket's melody—

Beneath the stars of heaven

1772

A picture in twilight and darkness.

Framed in loneliness—with regret for daily living.

It was this gray portrait

That brought forth my undoing.

Not from her beauty

But rather her *expression*—

Tinted by the same sadness I have known—

From the beginning.

407th Assembly

Jonathan Lovejoy

1773

Exhaustion rules the day—

When Failure comes my way

Every dream did live and die—

Despite what I had to pay

1774

I see the bluebird in the tree

He turns his head to look at me
The bluebird flies down to the ground
On top of my burial mound

The bluebird turns to look at me—
A ghost adrift in misery

1775

*T*hrough the windows of my prison—

The world passes me by

A whispered call from the future—

Where Hope begs tears to cry

1776

Before Indian Summer days

Birds speak of my demise

At the house by the Harvest Field

Divine delusion dies

Upon Autumn Rain's arrival

I gaze across the sea

Wondering why she never came

To sing my elegy

Jonathan Lovejoy

ABOUT THE AUTHOR

Jonathan Lovejoy is a graduate of the University of North Carolina at Greensboro with a B.A. in Religious Studies, and a graduate of Liberty University with an M.A. in Theological Studies. He currently lives in Winston Salem, North Carolina.

For more info on the author's life and career, visit jonathanlovejoy.com.